D0576581

GO GREEK!

Alison Hawes

Crabtree Publishing Company
www.crabtreebooks.com

Author: Alison Hawes
Editor: Kathy Middleton
Production coordinator: Ken Wright
Prepress technician: Margaret Amy Salter
Series consultant: Gill Matthews

Every effort has been made to trace copyright holders and to obtain their permission for use of copyright material. The authors and publishers would be pleased to rectify any error or omission in future editions. All the Internet addresses given in this book were correct at the time of going to press. The author and publishers regret any inconvenience caused if addresses have changed or sites have ceased to exist, but can accept no responsibility for any such changes.

Picture Credits:
Alamy Images: Ivy Close Images 18b
Alison Hawes: 5bl, 5bc, 7, 9, 11b, 13, 15, 17, 19, 21, 23, 25, 27, 29b
DK Images: (Cover) Liz McAulay
Fotolia: Denis Topal 6l
Istockphoto: Ulrich Schendzielorz 14t
The Ohio Statehouse Photo Archive: 16
Photolibrary: Gimmi Gimmi 24r
Shutterstock: Danilo Ascione 28b, Clara 28t, Panos Karapanagiotis 11t, 12r, Kompasstudio 4, Krechet 5t, Ninette Luz 2–32, Georgy Markov 20r, Ivan Montero Martinez 10, Maxstockphoto 18t, Michaela Stejskalova 8t, Florin Tirlea 8b
Wikimedia: Matthias Kabel 24l, Grant Mitchell 26t, Marie-Lan Nguyen 12l, 14b, 20l, 22b, 26b, Bibi Saint-Pol 6r, 22t, 29t
Map: Geoff Ward.

Library and Archives Canada Cataloguing in Publication

Hawes, Alison, 1952-
    Go Greek! / Alison Hawes.

(Crabtree connections)
Includes index.
ISBN 978-0-7787-9894-1 (bound).--ISBN 978-0-7787-9915-3 (pbk.)

4730 4946 10/11

    1. Greece--Civilization--To 146 B.C.--Juvenile literature.
2. Amusements--Greece--Juvenile literature. 3. Amusements--Juvenile literature. I. Title. II. Series: Crabtree connections

DF77.H39 2011   j938   C2010-905070-3

Library of Congress Cataloging-in-Publication Data

Hawes, Alison, 1952-
    Go Greek! / Alison Hawes.
       p. cm. -- (Crabtree connections)
    Includes index.
    ISBN 978-0-7787-9915-3 (pbk. : alk. paper) -- ISBN 978-0-7787-9894-1 (reinforced library binding : alk. paper)
    1. Greece--Civilization--To 146 B.C.--Juvenile literature. 2. Greece--Civilization--To 146 B.C.--Study and teaching (Elementary)--Activity programs. I. Title. II. Series.

DF77.H39 2011
938--dc22
                                                    2010030820

Crabtree Publishing Company
www.crabtreebooks.com   1-800-387-7650
Copyright © 2011 **CRABTREE PUBLISHING COMPANY.**
All rights reserved. No part of this publication may be reproduced, stored in a retrieval system or be transmitted in any form or by any means, electronic, mechanical, photocopying, recording, or otherwise, without the prior written permission of Crabtree Publishing Company. Published in the United Kingdom in 2010 by A & C Black Publishers Ltd. The right of the author of this work has been asserted.

Printed in the U.S.A./082010/WO20101210

Published in Canada
Crabtree Publishing
616 Welland Ave.
St. Catharines, Ontario
L2M 5V6

Published in the United States
Crabtree Publishing
PMB 59051
350 Fifth Avenue, 59th Floor
New York, New York 10118

Contents

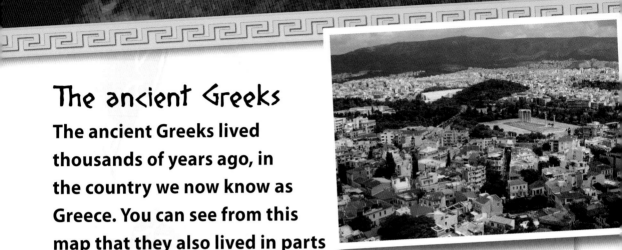

The ancient Greeks

The ancient Greeks lived thousands of years ago, in the country we now know as Greece. You can see from this map that they also lived in parts of modern day Italy and Turkey, as well as other countries.

Athens is the capital city of Greece.

FRANCE

ITALY

BULGARIA

ALBANIA

Aegean Sea

TURKEY

GREECE

•Athens

Ionian Sea

Mediterranean Sea

NORTH AFRICA

The places marked in orange on this map show where the ancient Greeks lived.

This temple was built in Athens in the 400s BC. Its ruins can still be visited today.

Archaeology

We know a lot about the ancient Greeks because archaeologists have found the remains of the temples, theaters, and ships they built. Many smaller items, such as pottery, jewelry, money, and toys, have also been discovered.

Have fun making your own ancient Greek items.

Activities

As well as information about the ancient Greeks, this book gives you instructions for different activities that you can do at home or at school. Enjoy the activities but DON'T FORGET THESE RULES:

- Read all the instructions before you begin.

- Protect yourself and the surface you are working on. (Some of the activities in the book are messy!)

- Always tidy up after you have completed an activity.

- Always ask for adult help when you see this **symbol**: *

The ancient Greeks were famous for making beautiful clay pots. We can learn a lot about the ancient Greeks from their pottery because they often decorated their pots with scenes from their everyday lives.

Pots with black pictures were first made in Corinth, around 700 BC.

The fashion for pots with red pictures began in Athens, in 530 BC.

Make your own Greek pot

You will need:

• *an old dinner plate* • *plastic wrap* • *short strips of newspaper and white paper* • *paste and paste brush* • *poster paints and paint brush* • *white glue*

1 Cover the upturned plate with plastic wrap.

2 Paste four layers of newspaper on top of this and leave to dry.

3 Paste two layers of white paper on top of this and again leave to dry.

4 Remove the dinner plate and plastic wrap.

5 Paste two layers of white paper on the inside of your paper plate.

6 When dry, paint a picture on your plate.

7 Finally, make your plate shiny by painting on a layer of white glue.

This finished plate has an ancient Greek design.

Shapes and sizes

About 20 different shapes were used to make ancient Greek pots.

You can tell by the shape of the pot what it was used for.

storing wine and oil

collecting water

pouring

drinking

7

Food

The ancient Greeks ate very healthily. They ate a lot of fruit and vegetables, bread, oatmeal, and sometimes fish. Only rich people could afford to eat a lot of meat.

The Greeks grew grapes to eat and also to make wine.

Ancient Greek menu

Breakfast:
bread dipped in wine

Lunch:
bread, cheese, and fruit

Dinner:
porridge or beans, and vegetables and bread

Pasteli is an ancient Greek treat made with honey and **sesame**.

The ancient Greeks used honey to sweeten their food. They kept their bees in clay hives.

Ask an adult for help when you see this sign.

Make your own pasteli*

You will need:

- *2/3 cup (150 ml) liquid honey*
- *2/3 cup (150 ml) sesame seeds*
- *a piece of lemon rind*
- *8-inch (20 cm) square baking pan (lined with wax paper)*
- *a medium saucepan*
- *kitchen scissors and wooden spoon*

1 Heat the honey in the saucepan until it starts to boil.

2 Stir in the lemon rind and the sesame seeds.

3 Simmer for a few minutes, stirring all the time.

4 Turn the heat off and remove the lemon rind.

5 Spread the mixture evenly in the baking pan and refrigerate for two hours.

6 Cut the pasteli into squares with kitchen scissors.

7 Peel the paper off and eat!

Store your pasteli on a plate in the fridge.

NOW TRY THIS!

The ancient Greeks cooked over an open fire—but you can use a stove. Find more ancient Greek recipes at the Web site below, and cook a meal for your friends.

www.greek-recipe.com/static/ancient/ancientrecipes.html

Theater

The ancient Greeks built many outdoor theaters. They went to the theater to see plays, music, and dancing.

Actors in Greek plays wore masks. The masks showed the audience the kind of character the actor was playing. Plays from ancient Greece are still sometimes performed today.

No women!

All the actors in ancient Greek plays were men. They played the women's roles, too.

This theater was in Epidaurus, Greece, and held about 14,000 people.

Make your own theater mask*

You will need:

• a balloon • plastic wrap • a small roll of plaster of paris bandages cut into short lengths • scissors • poster paints and paint brush • pencil

1 Blow up the balloon to the same size as your head.

2 Wrap the balloon in plastic wrap.

3 Dip the bandage strips into water one at a time. Cover one side of the balloon with two layers of bandages.

4 Let the mask dry and remove the balloon and plastic wrap.

5 Draw eyes and a mouth on the mask, and cut them out.

6 Add another layer of bandages to your mask.

7 Then use more bandage strips to make eyebrows, lips, cheeks, and a nose that stand out from the face.

8 Let dry before painting.

Greek plays were either tragedies or comedies. This sad mask is designed for a Greek tragedy.

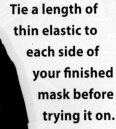

Tie a length of thin elastic to each side of your finished mask before trying it on.

Almost every year, a big sports festival would
be held somewhere in ancient Greece. The most
famous festival was the **Olympic Games** held at
Olympia. Only men were
allowed to take part.
Women were not
even allowed
to watch.

Athletics was a favorite
Greek pastime.

Winners of sports
competitions were often
awarded victory wreaths
and wool ribbons.

Make your own victory wreath*

You will need:

- *medium garden wire*
- *green electrical tape*
- *green paper*
- *scissors*

1 Measure your head and cut twice this length of garden wire.

2 Form the wire into a double ring.

3 Wrap the tape all the way around the ring, until the wire is hidden.

4 Cut 40 life-size leaves with short stalks from the green paper.

5 Starting at the top, tape a leaf to the wire by its stalk.

6 Next, work backward down one side of the ring, and tape more leaves on, each one overlapping the one before.

7 When you have covered half of the ring, go back up to the top and cover the other side of the ring with leaves.

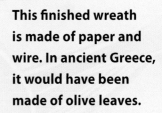

This finished wreath is made of paper and wire. In ancient Greece, it would have been made of olive leaves.

For women

Women had their own sports festival. It was held in honor of the goddess Hera.

13

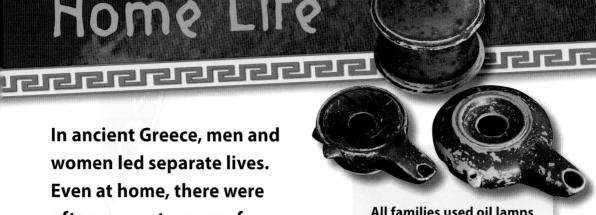

In ancient Greece, men and women led separate lives. Even at home, there were often separate rooms for men and women.

All families used oil lamps to light their homes.

Women and girls were expected to spend most of their time at home. Women who came from rich families had slaves to do most household chores for them. Women from poor families had to do all the work themselves.

It was a woman's job to spin and weave the cloth needed to make her family's clothes.

14

Make a decorative oil lamp*

You will need:

- *10 ounces (300 g) of self-hardening clay*
- *a workboard*
- *a drinking straw*
- *plastic wrap*

1 Wrap a quarter of the clay in plastic wrap.

2 Roll the remaining clay into a ball.

3 Flatten the ball slightly and then push both your thumbs into the middle.

4 Hollow out the middle of the ball with your hands.

5 As you work, make a handle at one end of the lamp and a lip for the nozzle at the other end.

Ancient Greeks would push a wick into the nozzle and pour a little olive oil into the lamp. The wick would then be lit.

6 When the base is finished, take the first clay out of the plastic wrap and roll it into a ball.

7 Flatten it out into a large, thick circle to make a lid for your lamp.

8 Make a hole in the lid with a straw.

9 Join the lid to the base by pressing them together with your fingers.

10 Leave your decorative lamp to dry completely.

15

Law

The ancient Greeks first introduced the idea of having a **jury** in a **court of law**. A **water clock** was used in the courts to limit the time people could speak.

Being on a jury

In Athens, **citizens** were expected to serve on a jury. To serve on a jury you had to be

- born in Athens;
- over 30 years old;
- a man.

The jury voted whether someone was guilty or innocent of a crime. **Jurors** were given two **ballot** tokens to vote with.

ΚΛΕΙΣΘΕΜΗΣ

Democratic Greece

All men in ancient Greece could vote. The system in which all citizens can vote is called democracy. It was introduced by Cleisthenes (above). However, only men could vote in ancient Greece.

16

Make your own ballot tokens

You will need:

- *a plastic bottle cap*
- *thick card stock*
- *a drinking straw*
- *self-hardening clay*
- *bronze paint and paint brush*
- *single-hole punch*

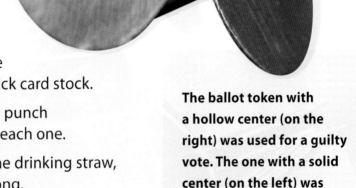

1 Trace a line around the bottle cap twice on thick card stock.

2 Cut the circles out and punch a hole in the center of each one.

3 Cut two pieces from the drinking straw, each 2 inches (5 cm) long.

4 Push a cut straw halfway through each circle.

5 Plug both ends of only one straw with clay and leave to dry.

6 Give each token three coats of bronze paint.

The ballot token with a hollow center (on the right) was used for a guilty vote. The one with a solid center (on the left) was used for a not guilty vote.

NOW TRY THIS!

Ancient Greek juries had hundreds of members. Find out how many people are on a jury today. Is it the same as it was in Athens?

The ancient Greeks thought education was important. Wealthy families sent their sons to school when they were seven. Boys studied reading, writing, math, music, poetry, and sports. They wrote on **wax tablets**. Poor boys didn't usually go to school, and girls were taught at home by their mothers.

Ancient Greeks wrote on scrolls made of **papyrus** or animal skin.

This piece of an ancient pot shows students and their teachers. The students are being taught to read and play music.

Make your own scroll*

You will need:

- *large wooden dowel*
- *4 small decorative drawer knobs*
- *wood glue*
- *a short roll of paper*
- *cold tea*
- *double-sided sticky tape*
- *paper towels*

1 Cut two 9-inch (23 cm) rollers from the wooden dowel.

2 Glue the drawer knobs to the ends of the rollers and leave overnight to dry.

3 Make a pot of strong black tea, and let it go cold.

4 Pour the tea into a bowl and dip the roll of paper in it for a few seconds.

5 Let the paper dry on paper towels overnight.

6 Attach the ends of the roll of paper to the rollers with sticky tape.

Roll up your finished scroll when not in use and tie it with a ribbon or elastic band.

Α Β Γ Δ Ε Ζ Η Θ Ι
Κ Λ Μ Ν Ξ Ο Π Ρ Σ
Τ Υ Φ Χ Ψ Ω

NOW TRY THIS!

Use the link below to copy the Greek alphabet on to your scroll or try writing your name in Greek letters:

http://www.schoolhistory. co.uk/primarylinks/ancient greeceresources/greece17.pdf

Ancient Greeks wore two main pieces of clothing—a tunic and a cloak. Tunics could be short or long and were fastened at the shoulders. They were usually made of cotton or silk.

Cloaks were wrapped around the body or pinned at one shoulder.

The tunics worn by women were usually longer than those worn by men.

Make your own Greek clothes

You will need:

- *3 to 4½ feet (1 m to 1.5 m) of fabric for the cloak and a large rectangle of fabric for the tunic*
- *peel-and-stick Velcro*
- *6 feet (2 m) of colored cord*
- *needle and thread*
- *scissors*

1 To make the tunic, get someone to measure the distance between your wrists with your arms held stretched out to the sides. Double that number. Then measure the distance from your shoulder to your feet.

2 Cut a rectangle of fabric matching these measurements and fold it in half widthwise.

3 Sew up the side seam.

4 Tape pieces of Velcro along the top edge, spacing them so there is room for your arms and head when fastened.

5 Put the tunic on, press the Velcro fasteners together, and tie the cord around your waist as a belt.

6 Pull some of the tunic up, so it hangs over the cord belt.

7 To make the cloak, fold the fabric lengthwise and wrap it around your body, fastening it at the shoulder with a broach or Velcro.

This tunic is called a chiton.

Toys and Games

Children in ancient Greece liked to play games and take part in sports. Younger children may have played with toys, such as spinning tops. Spinning tops were made from clay or wood. Children would make them spin by pulling a strip of leather.

Older children may have played with toys, such as yo-yos or marbles. They especially loved games with scary names, like "knucklebones."

This plate shows a Greek child playing with a yo-yo.

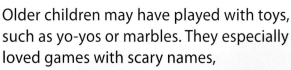

This pull toy from ancient Greece is over 2,500 years old.

Make your own knucklebones game

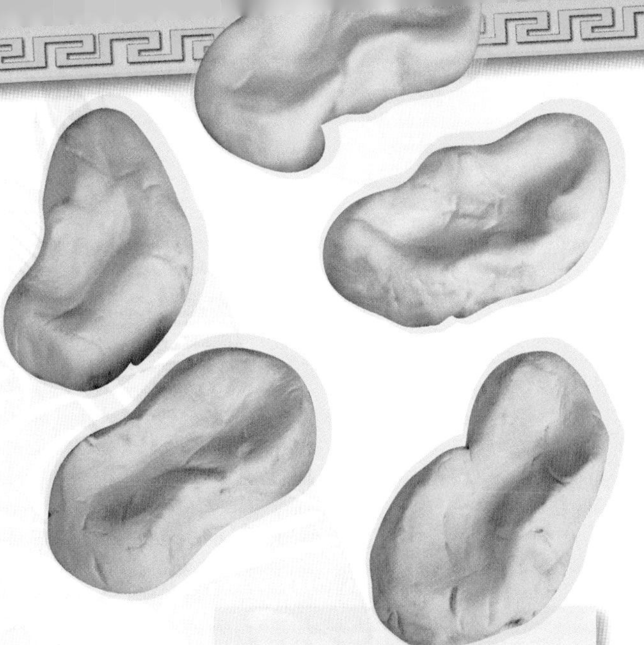

You will need:

- *1 ounce (25 g) of self-hardening clay*
- *workboard*
- *white- or cream-colored paint*

1 Cut the clay into 5 pieces and roll each one into a ball.

2 Using your fingers, slightly flatten and squeeze each ball into a knucklebone shape.

3 Mark the knucklebones with dents and ridges, like the knucklebones in the photograph above right.

4 Leave the "bones" to dry completely.

5 Give the knucklebones three coats of white or cream paint.

The ancient Greeks used ankle bones from sheep and goats as "knucklebones." They also made them from clay, like the ones shown above.

NOW TRY THIS!

No one is quite sure how the ancient Greeks played the game of knucklebones. It is thought the rules may have been like those for Fives or Jacks.

Visit www.mastersgames.com/rules/jacks-rules.htm to find out how to play and challenge a friend to a game.

No place in Greece is far from the sea. So it is not surprising that the ancient Greeks became great sailors and shipbuilders. In the 500s BC, the ancient Greeks invented a new warship called a trireme.
They were powered by sails and 170 oarsmen.

Protective eye

Many ships had a large eye painted on the **prow**. Ancient Greeks believed it protected their ship from bad luck and from their enemies.

A trireme had a long metal spike on its prow. It was used as a **battering ram** against enemy ships.

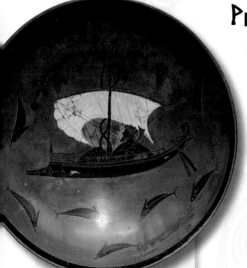

Greek ships carried olive oil, pots, and wine to countries all around the Mediterranean Sea.

Make your own protective eye

You will need:

- *poster paints and paint brush*
- *a large paper plate*
- *a piece of ribbon*
- *sticky tape*
- *thick black marker*

Bold colors and a dark outline make the eye stand out.

1 Paint a large eye in the center circle of the plate.

2 Paint a plain background around the eye.

3 Paint the border of the plate in a different color.

4 When the border is dry, draw a pattern on it with the marker.

5 Outline the eye with the marker.

6 Tape a loop of ribbon on to the back of the plate and hang it in your room.

The border surrounding this plate has a "key" pattern. The design was very popular in ancient Greece.

NOW TRY THIS!

Did you know there was nowhere to sleep or eat on a trireme? Watch a great video about triremes at:

www.youtube.com/watch?v=A46UCkZRnoM&NR=1

Find out more about triremes at:

www.historyforkids.org/learn/greeks/science/sailing/warships.htm

Greek men were expected to serve in the army.
Most fought as foot soldiers called hoplites.

Hoplite
soldiers
marched into
battle with
their shields
overlapping
and their
spears ready
to throw.

To protect his body a
soldier carried a large
shield and wore a helmet,
a **cuirass**, and **greaves**.

Make your own hoplite shield

You will need:

- *a large sheet of thick white card stock*
- *a large sheet of thin black card stock*
- *white glue and paste brush*
- *poster paints and brush*
- *scissors*
- *paper clips*

1 Cut out a 20-inch (51 cm) wide circle out of the white card stock for the shield.

2 Draw 2 circles on the shield, one inside the other. Make one 17-inches (45 cm) wide and the other 16-inches (41 cm) wide.

3 Paint a design in the center of your shield.

4 Paint the border between the 16-inch (41 cm) and 17-inch (45 cm) circles and leave to dry.

5 Cut flaps at 2-inch (5 cm) intervals, from the edge of the 20-inch (51 cm) circle to the edge of the 17-inch (45 cm) circle, and fold them back.

6 Glue a strip of black card stock to the flaps to form a rim around the shield. Hold the strip in place with paper clips until dry.

7 Glue a short strip of card stock to the inside of the shield to make a handle and leave to dry.

The painting on this finished card shield shows the snake-haired Medusa from Greek legend.

27

Myths and Legends

The ancient Greeks told countless stories about their gods and heroes. We know these **myths and legends** today because the Greeks wrote them down.

Some Greek myths can also be seen painted as **friezes** on pots or carved into stone.

One of the most famous Greek legends tells how the hero Perseus killed the snake-haired Medusa (above).

There are many stories of the Greek hero **Heracles**. This statue shows him fighting a centaur, who was part man and part horse.

Make your own story frieze

You will need:

- *a book of Greek myths and legends*
- *4 or 5 sheets of white paper*
- *felt-tip pens*
- *colored bristol board*
- *scissors*
- *glue stick*

1 Choose your favorite Greek myth or legend.

2 Decide on four or five important scenes to tell your story.

3 Draw each scene on one of the white sheets of paper.

4 Color your pictures with felt-tip pens.

5 Mount the finished frieze on the bristol board.

6 Decorate the border with a Greek pattern copied from a vase.

This Greek pot shows brave Theseus about to kill the Minotaur, who was part man and part bull.

The story in this frieze shows how Theseus sailed to Crete to defeat the Minotaur.

Glossary

ballot A vote

battering ram A thick, heavy pole used to break through an enemy's defenses

citizen A person who lives in a place and is allowed to vote there

court of law A building or room where a judge and jury make their decision

cuirass Bronze or leather armor protecting the upper body

frieze A picture or decoration running around the sides of a pot or a building

greaves Leg protectors

Heracles In Greek myths, he was the strongest man on Earth

jurors People who serve on a jury

jury A group of people who decide whether someone is innocent or guilty in a lawcourt

Medusa A female monster with snakes for hair who turned those who looked at her into stone

myths Ancient stories about gods, goddesses, and heroes

Olympic Games In ancient Greece, these games were held every four years for five days, in honor of the god Zeus

papyrus A type of paper made from plant stems

Perseus In Greek myths he was the son of Zeus

prow The front, pointed end of a ship

sesame A plant with tiny edible seeds

symbol A pattern or picture

water clock A small vessel with a hole in the side used to measure a speaker's time in court. When the water would run out of the hole, the speaker's time was up.

wax tablet A piece of wood with a wax covering, on which people wrote

wreath A ring of leaves or flowers worn on the head

Further Information

Web sites

This Web site links you to other Web sites about ancient Greece. Click on Ancient Greece for Kids at:
www.kidskonnect.com/content/view/254/27/

Find out all about the theater in ancient Greece at:
www.ancientgreece.co.uk/festivals/explore/exp_set.html

Find out who's who in the world of the Greek gods at:
http://greece.mrdonn.org/greekgods/index.html

This excellent Web site from Tufts University in the United States is filled with material about the ancient Olympics. The sections on Athletes' Stories and A Tour of Ancient Olympia are especially good. Find them at:
www.perseus.tufts.edu/Olympics/

Books

Hail! Ancient Greeks (Hail! History) by Jen Green. Crabtree Publishing (2011).

Life in Ancient Greece (Peoples of the Ancient World) by Lynn Peppas. Crabtree Publishing Company (2004).

How to Be an Ancient Greek Athlete by Jacqueline Morley. National Geographic Children's Books (2008).

Index